HAL•LEONARD®

GUITAR
PLAY-ALONG

AUDIO
ACCESS
INCLUDED

PLAYBACK+
Speed • Pitch • Balance • Loop

THE
DOOBIE
BROTHERS

VOL. 172

T0079127

Cover photo © Clayton Call/Redferns

To access audio visit:
www.halleonard.com/mylibrary

Enter Code
6301-0413-1774-5035

ISBN 978-1-4803-4462-4

Visit Hal Leonard Online at
www.halleonard.com

Contact Us:
Hal Leonard
7777 West Bluemound Road
Milwaukee, WI 53213
Email: info@halleonard.com

In Europe contact:
Hal Leonard Europe Limited
Distribution Centre, Newmarket Road
Bury St Edmunds, Suffolk, IP33 3YB
Email: info@halleonardeurope.com

In Australia contact:
Hal Leonard Australia Pty. Ltd.
4 Lentara Court
Cheltenham, Victoria, 3192 Australia
Email: info@halleonard.com.au

CONTENTS

Black Water

Words and Music by Patrick Simmons

Double drop D tuning:
(low to high) D-A-D-G-B-D

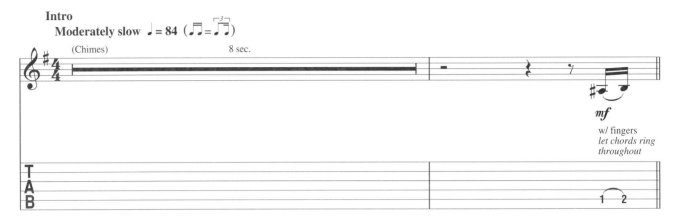

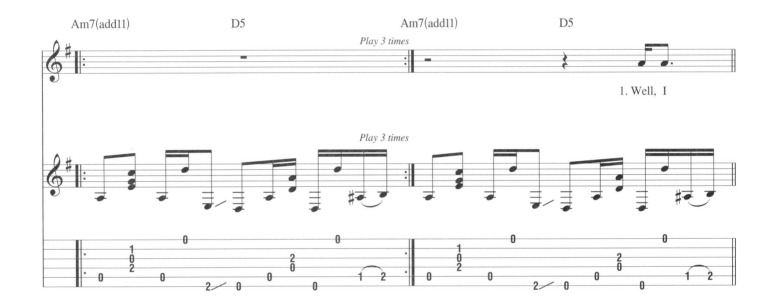

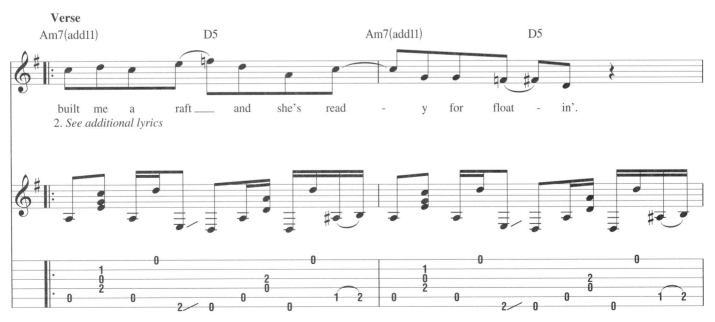

Ol' Mis - sis - sip - pi, _____ she's _ call - in' my name. _

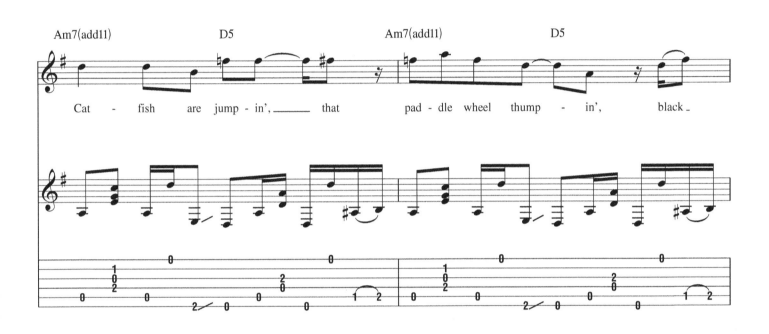

Cat - fish are jump - in', _____ that pad - dle wheel thump - in', black _

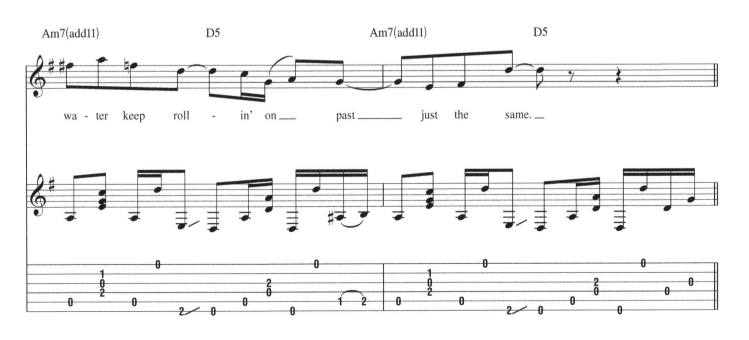

wa - ter keep roll - in' on __ past _____ just the same. _

Chorus

Mis - sis - sip - pi moon, won't ya keep on shin - in' on
(Old black wa - ter, keep on roll - in'.

me.
(Old black wa - ter, keep on roll - in'.

Mis - sis - sip - pi moon, won't ya keep on shin - in' on

me.
(Old black wa - ter, keep on roll - in'.

Mis - sis - sip - pi moon, won't ya keep on shin - in' on

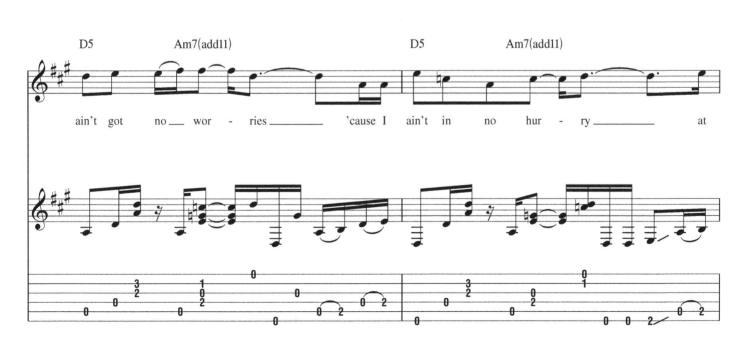

all.

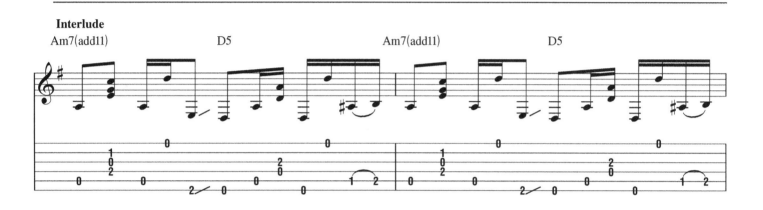

Interlude

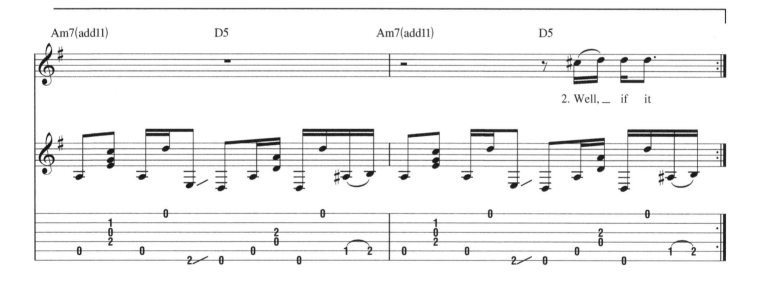

2. Well, __ if it

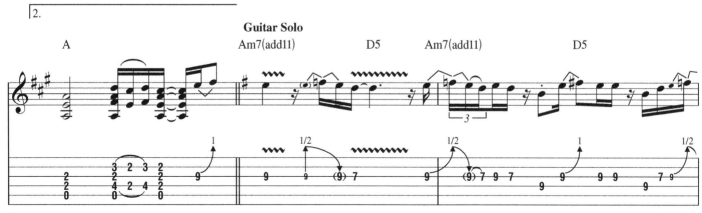

Guitar Solo

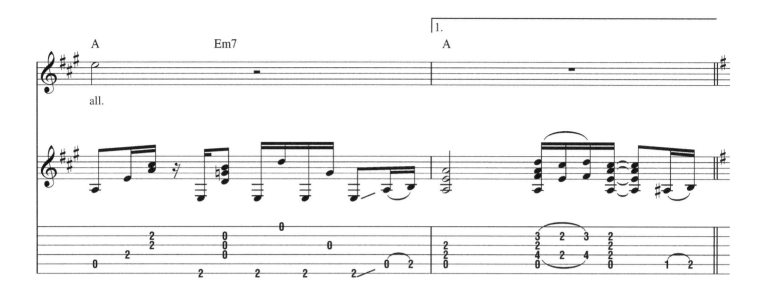

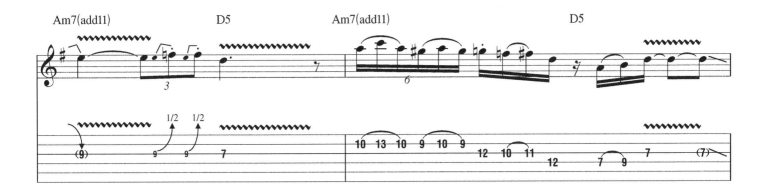

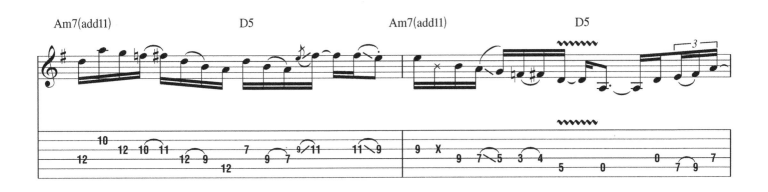

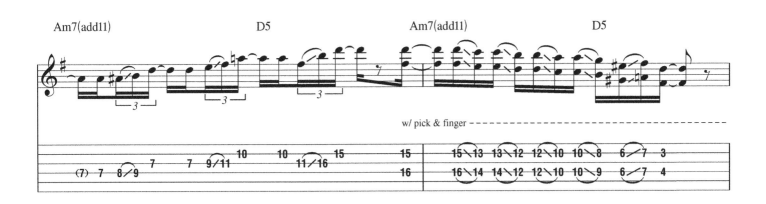

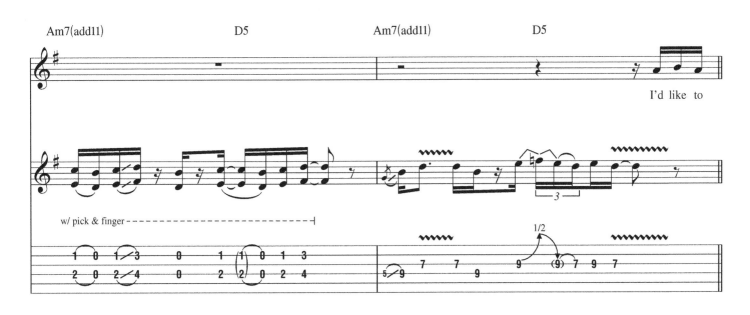

Outro

*Fade out over next 4 meas.

hear some funk - y Dix - ie - land,_ pret - ty ma - ma come and take me by the hand._

By the

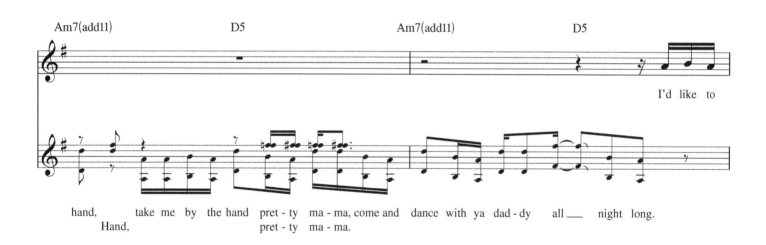

hand, take me by the hand pret - ty ma - ma, come and dance with ya dad - dy all _ night long.
Hand, pret - ty ma - ma.

I'd like to

Gtr. tacet
N.C.

hear some funk - y Dix - ie - land,_ pret - ty ma - ma come and take me by the hand._

By the

I wan - na

I'd like to

hand,   take me by the hand pret - ty ma - ma, come and dance with ya dad - dy all ___ night long.

Hand,   pret - ty ma - ma.

honk - y tonk,   honk - y tonk,   honk - y tonk   with you all night long.

Am7(add11)   D5

hear some funk - y Dix - ie - land, ___ pret - ty ma - ma come and take me by the hand. ___

By the

I wan - na

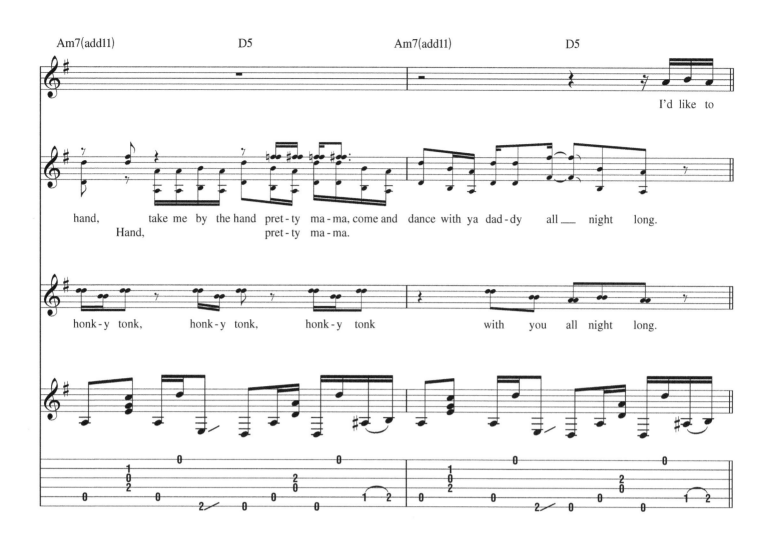

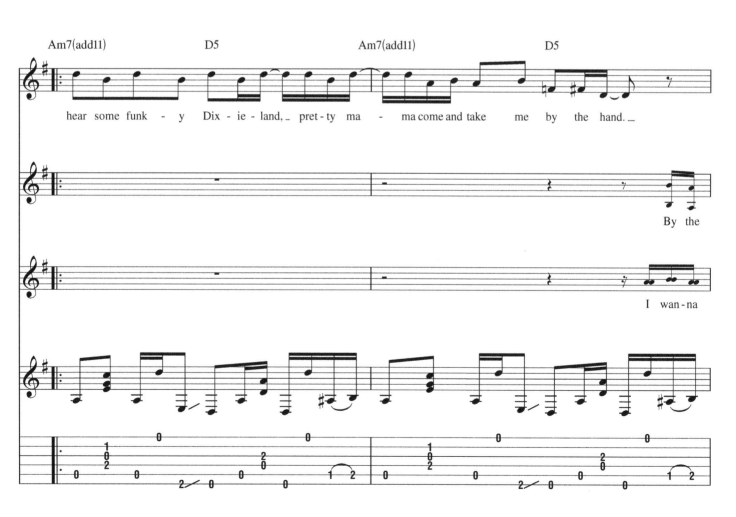

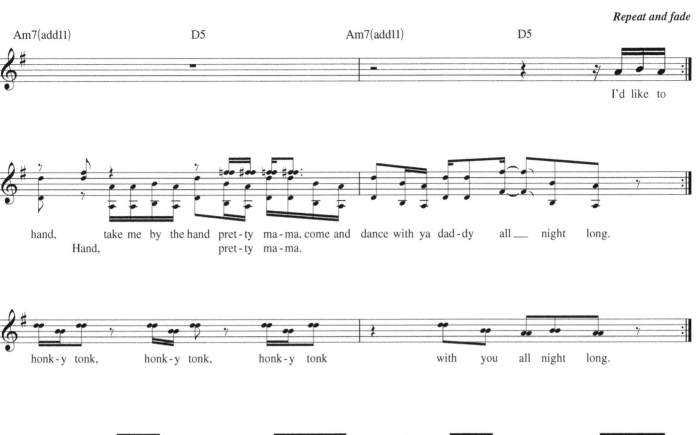

Additional Lyrics

2. Well, if it rains I don't care,
   Don't make no difference to me,
   Just take that streetcar that's goin' uptown.
   Yeah, I'd like to hear some funky Dixieland
   And dance a honky tonk
   And I'll be buy'n' ev'rybody drinks all around.

China Grove

Words and Music by Tom Johnston

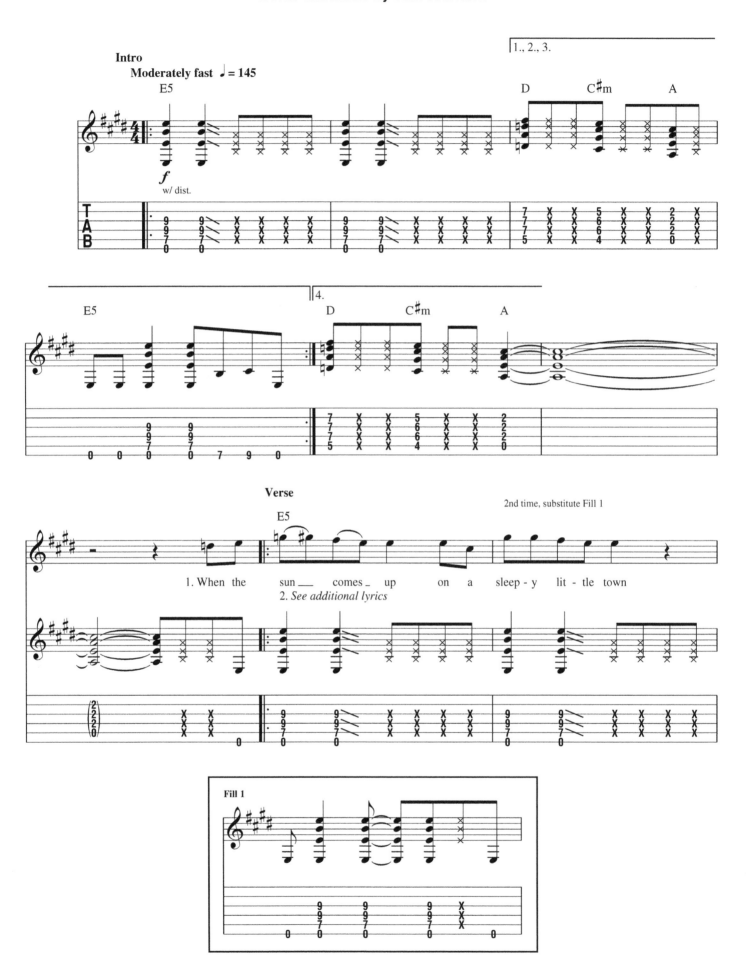

1. When the sun ___ comes ___ up on a sleep - y lit - tle town

2. *See additional lyrics*

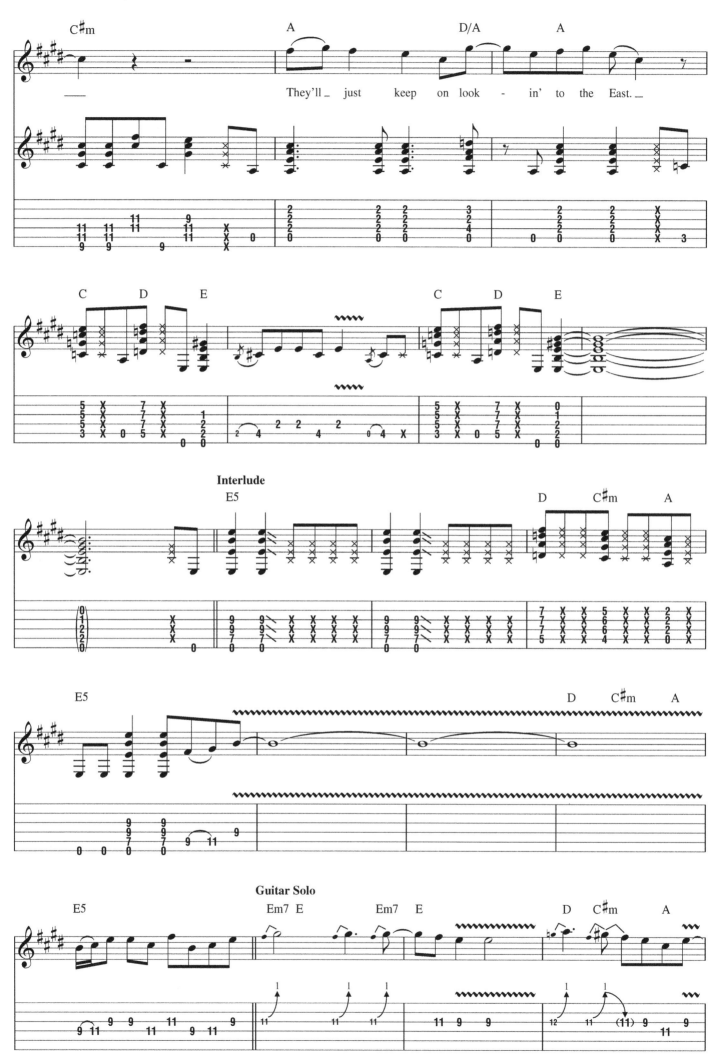

They'll _ just keep on look - in' to the East. _

Additional Lyrics

2. Well, the preacher and the teacher, Lord, they're a caution.
   They are the talk of the town.
   When the gossip gets to flyin' and they ain't lyin' when the sun go crawlin' down.
   They say that the father's insane and dear Missus Perkin's a game.

Jesus Is Just Alright

Words and Music by Arthur Reynolds

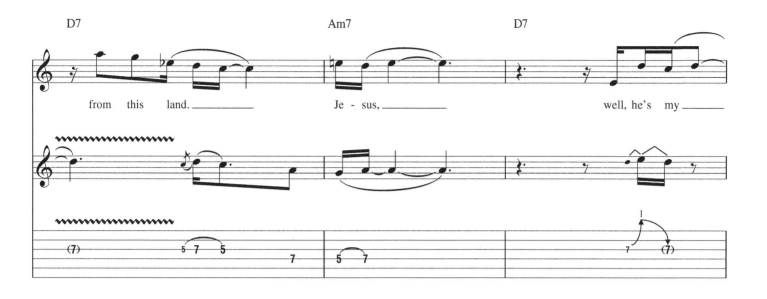

from this land. _____ Je - sus, _____ well, he's my _____

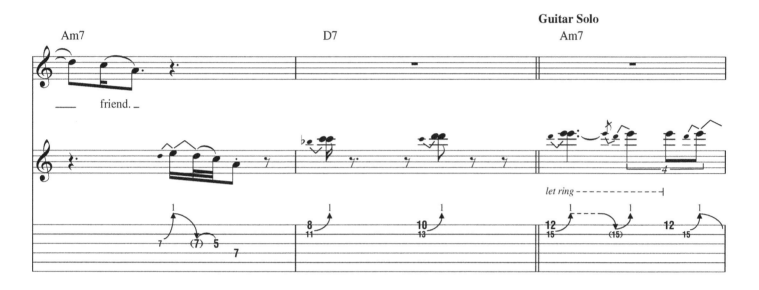

friend. ___

Guitar Solo

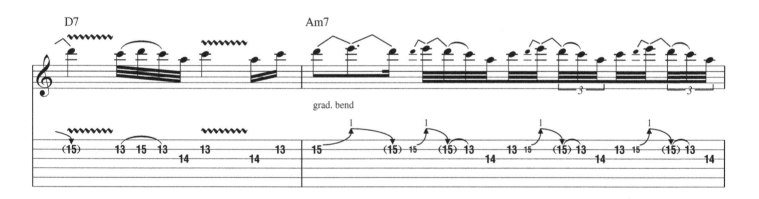

grad. bend

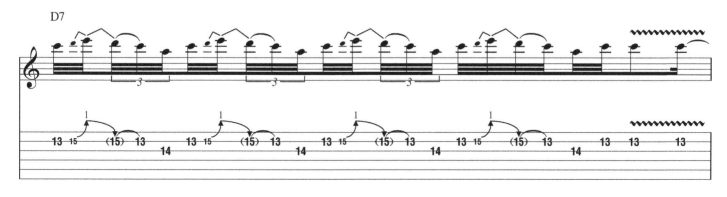

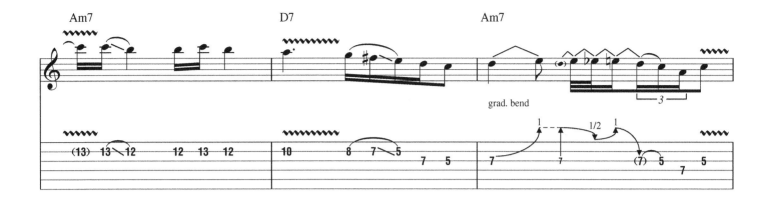

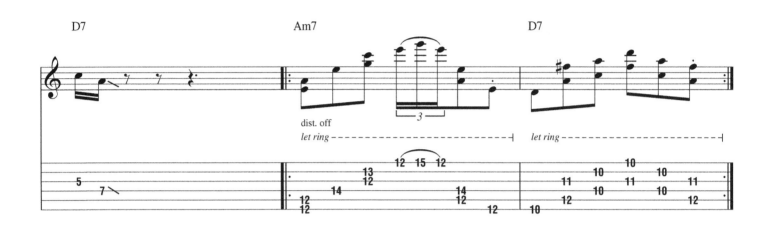

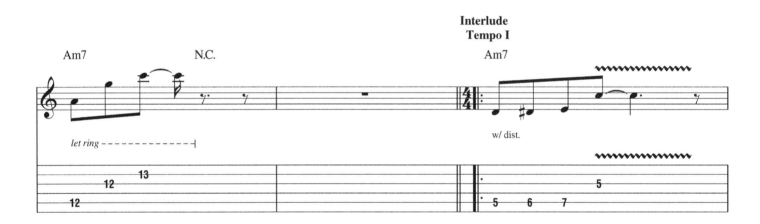

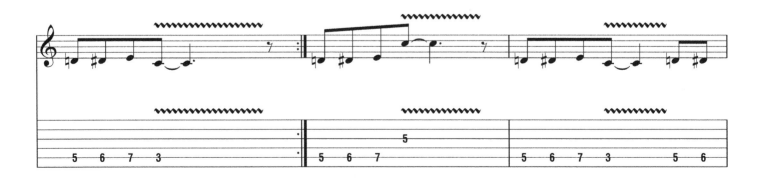

Guitar Solo

Am7

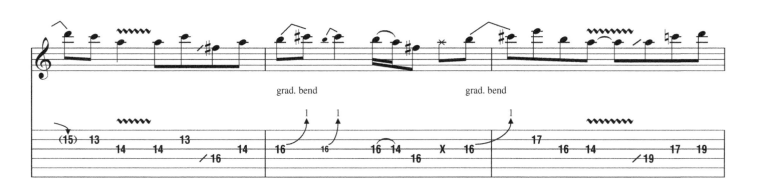

D.S. al Coda 2

⊕ Coda 2

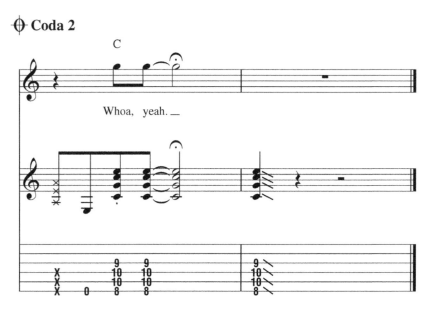

Whoa, yeah. __

Listen to the Music

Words and Music by Tom Johnston

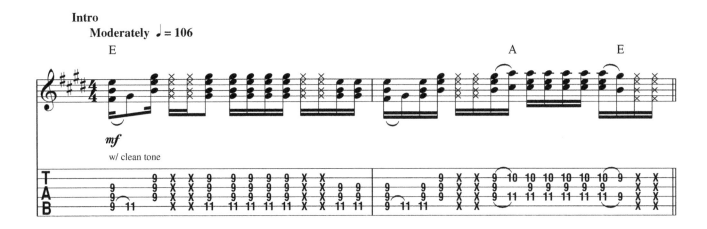

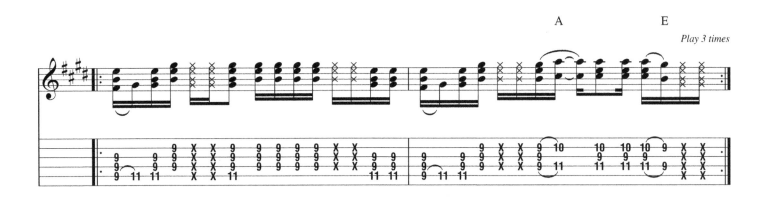

% **Verse**

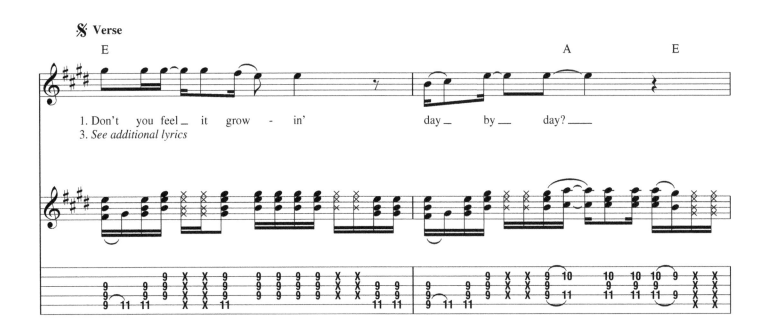

1. Don't you feel ___ it grow - in' day ___ by ___ day? ___
3. *See additional lyrics*

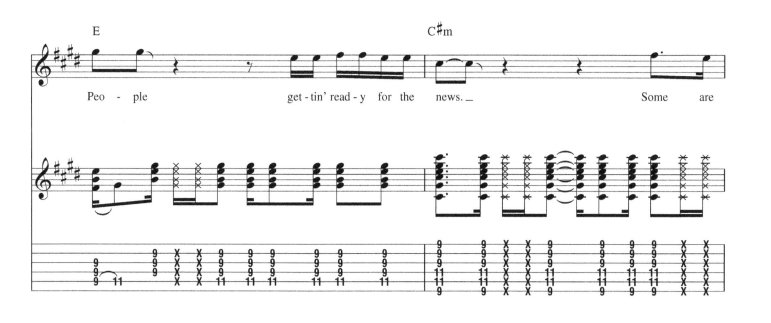

People get-tin' read-y for the news. ___ Some are

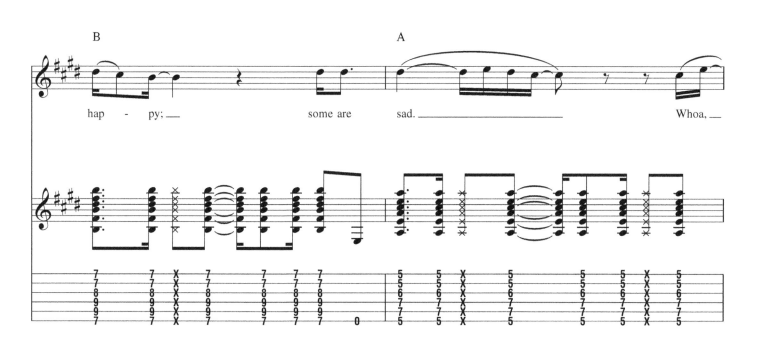

hap - py; ___ some are sad. ___ Whoa, ___

___ we're gon-na let the mu - sic play. ___

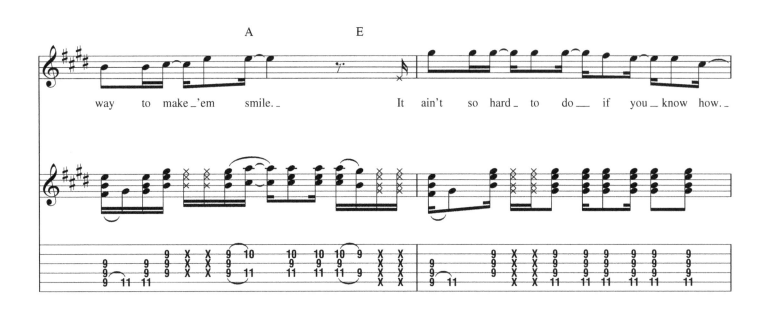

through. _____ Lord, __ now, ma - ma, go - in' to af - ter 'while. _

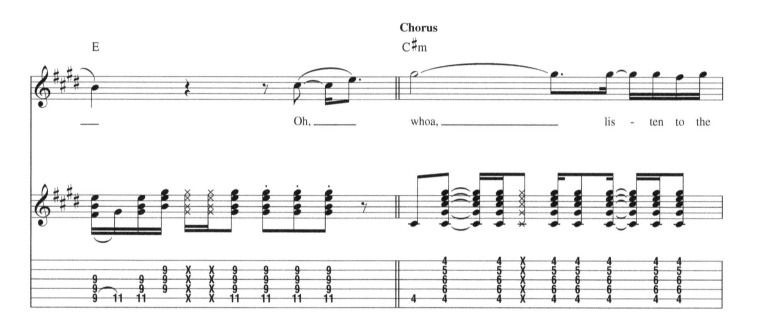

Chorus

__ Oh, _____ whoa, _____ lis - ten to the

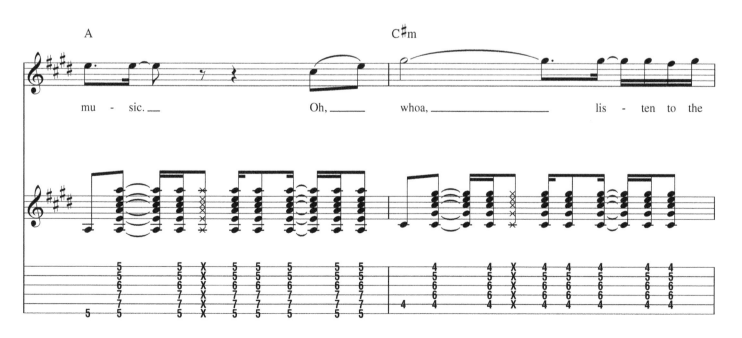

mu - sic. __ Oh, _____ whoa, _____ lis - ten to the

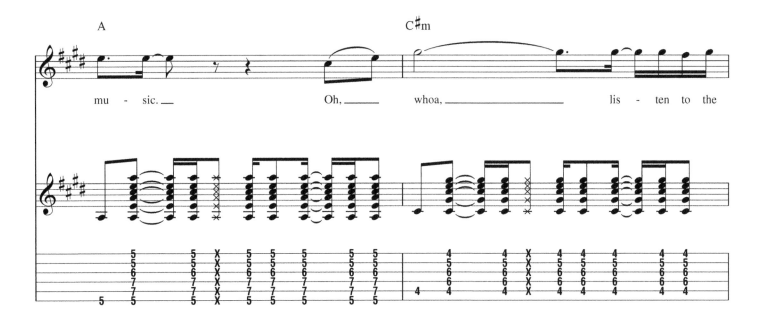

music. ___ Oh, ___ whoa, _____ lis - ten to the

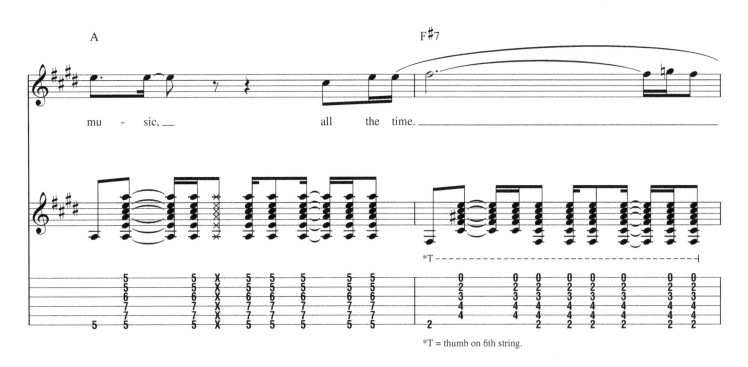

music, ___ all the time. _____

*T = thumb on 6th string.

To Coda ⊕

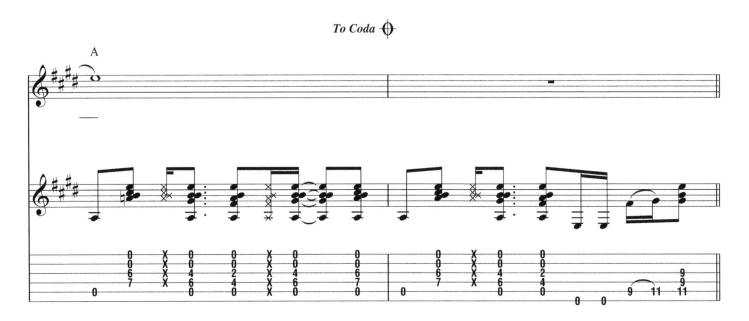

Interlude

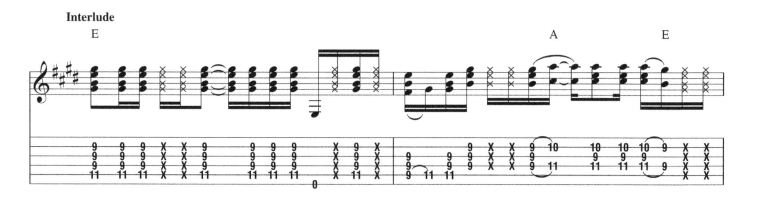

D.S. al Coda

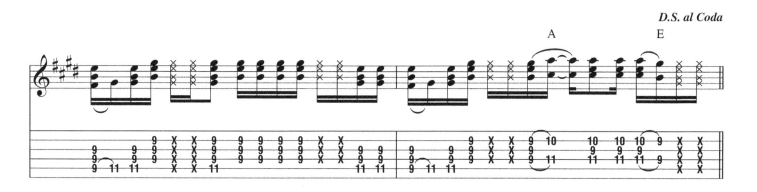

⊕ **Coda**

Bridge

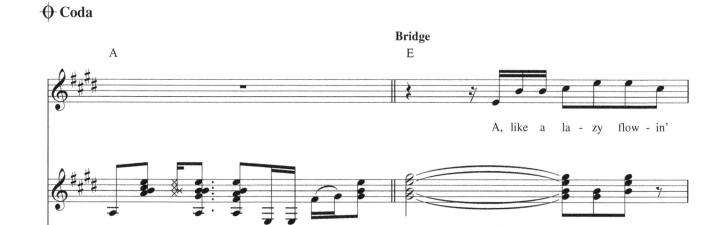

A, like a la - zy flow - in'

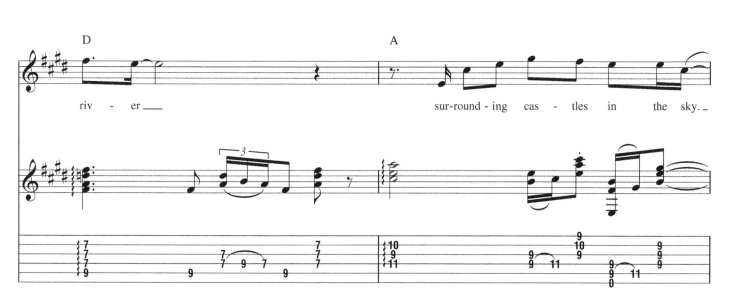

riv - er____   sur-round - ing cas - tles in the sky.__

And the crowd is grow-ing big - ger

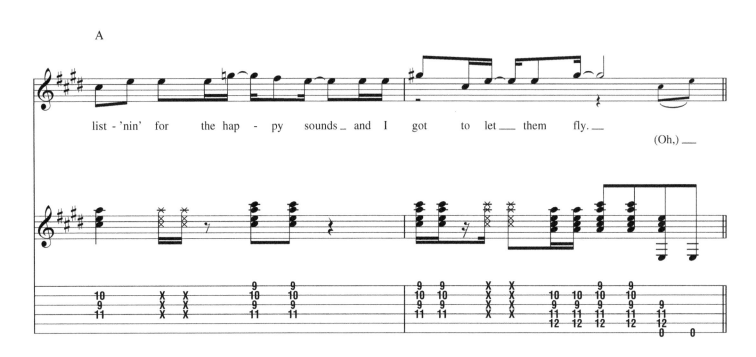

list - 'nin' for the hap - py sounds _ and I got to let _ them fly. _

(Oh,) _

Outro-Chorus

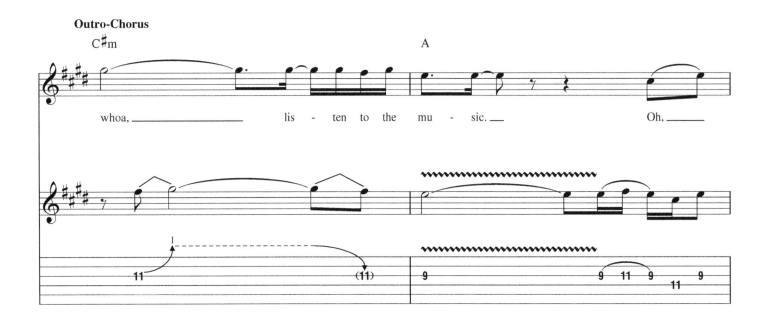

whoa, _____ lis - ten to the mu - sic. _ Oh, _____

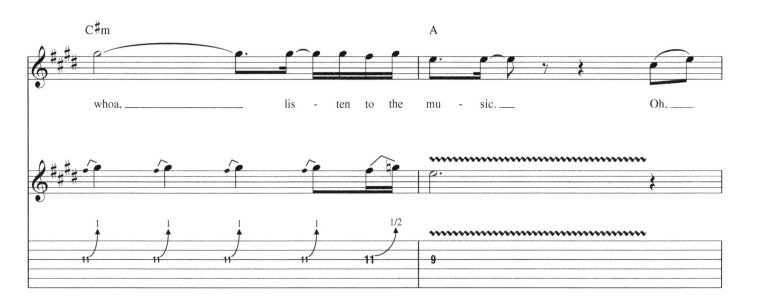

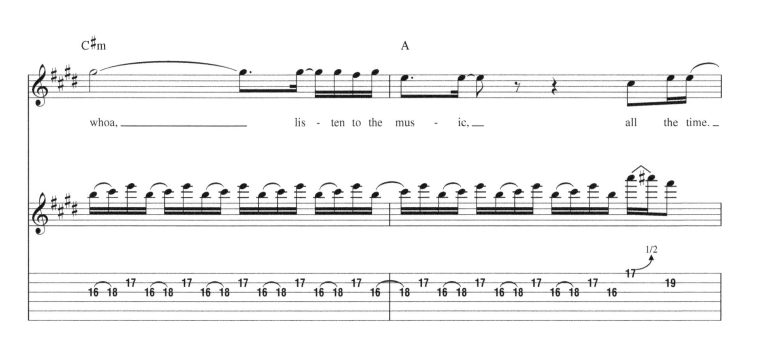

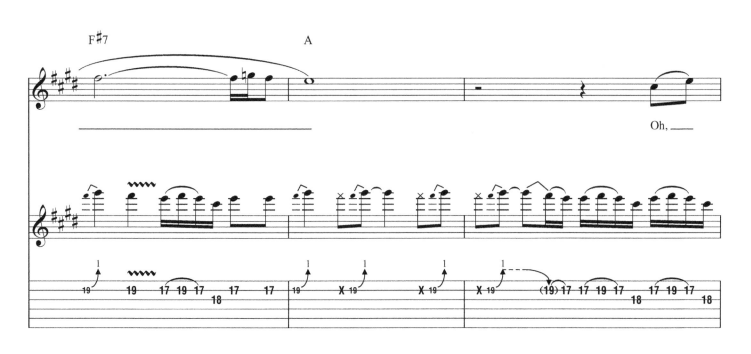

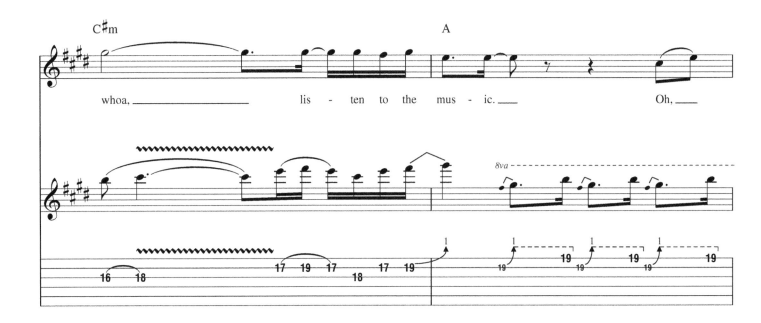

whoa,_____ lis - ten to the mus - ic.___ Oh,___

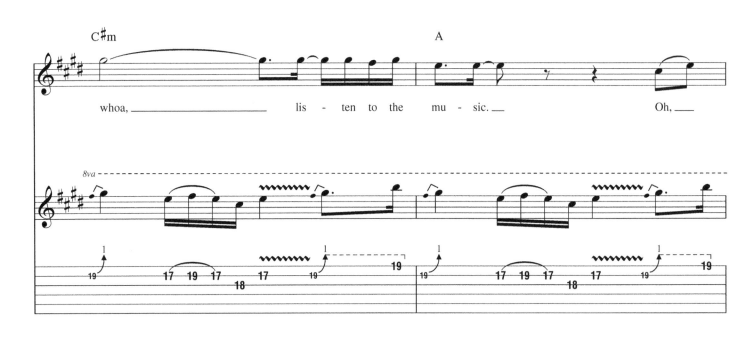

whoa,_____ lis - ten to the mu - sic.___ Oh,___

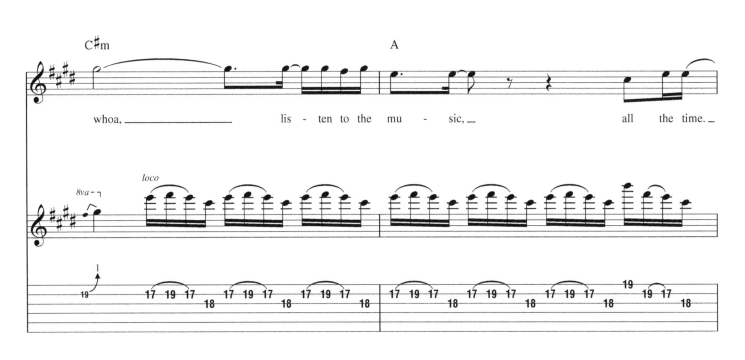

whoa,_____ lis - ten to the mu - sic,___ all the time.___

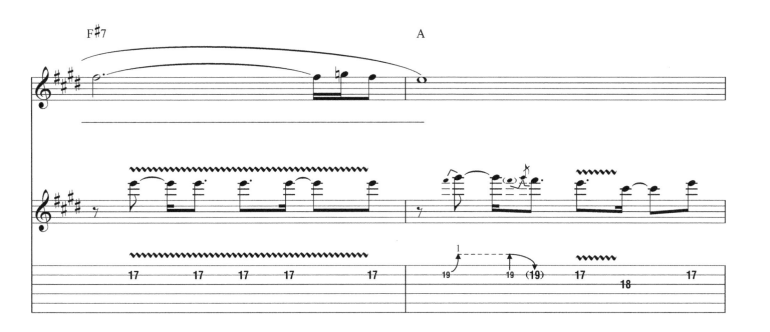

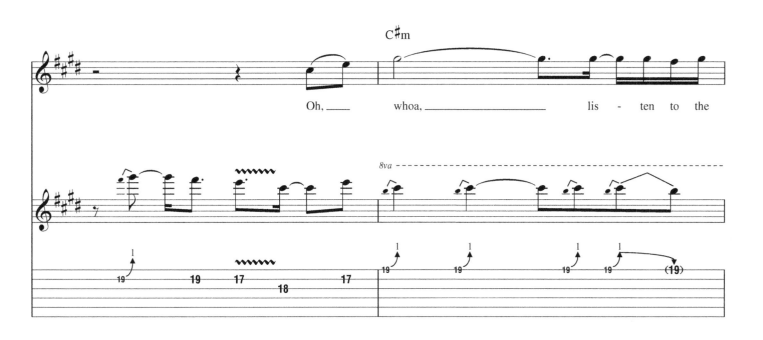

Oh, _____ whoa, _____ lis - ten to the

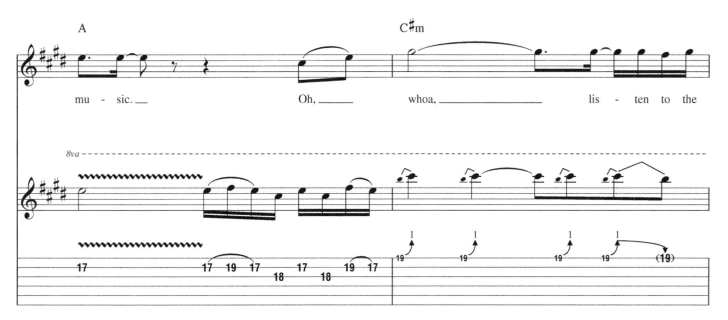

mu - sic. ___ Oh, _____ whoa, _____ lis - ten to the

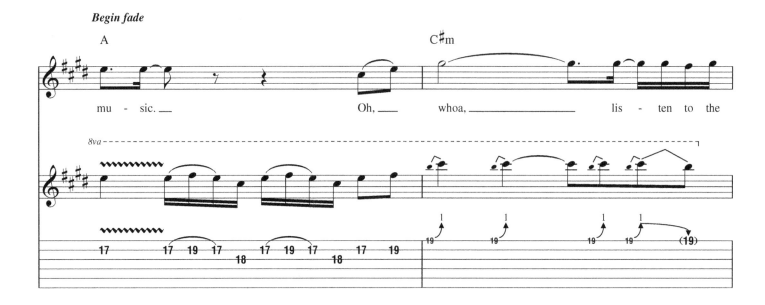

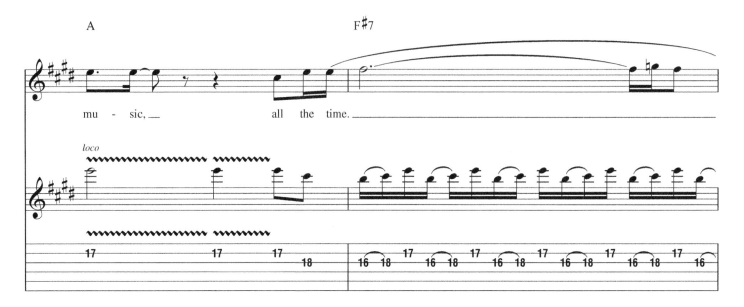

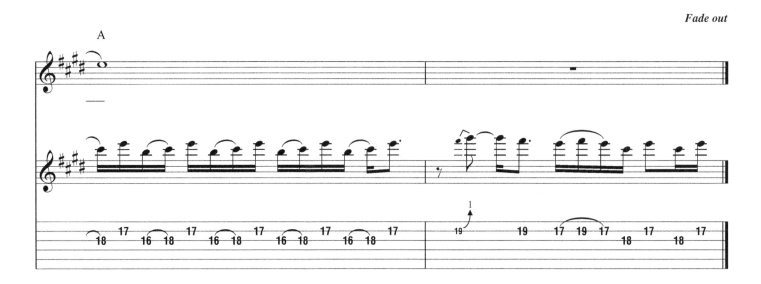

Additional Lyrics

3. Well, I know you know better, ev'rything I say.
   Meet me in the country for a day.
   We'll be happy, and we'll dance, Lord,
   We're gonna dance the blues away.

4. But, if I'm feelin' good to you and you're feelin' good to me,
   There ain't nothin' we can't do or say.
   Feelin' good, feelin' fine.
   Whoa, baby, let the music play.

Long Train Runnin'

Words and Music by Tom Johnston

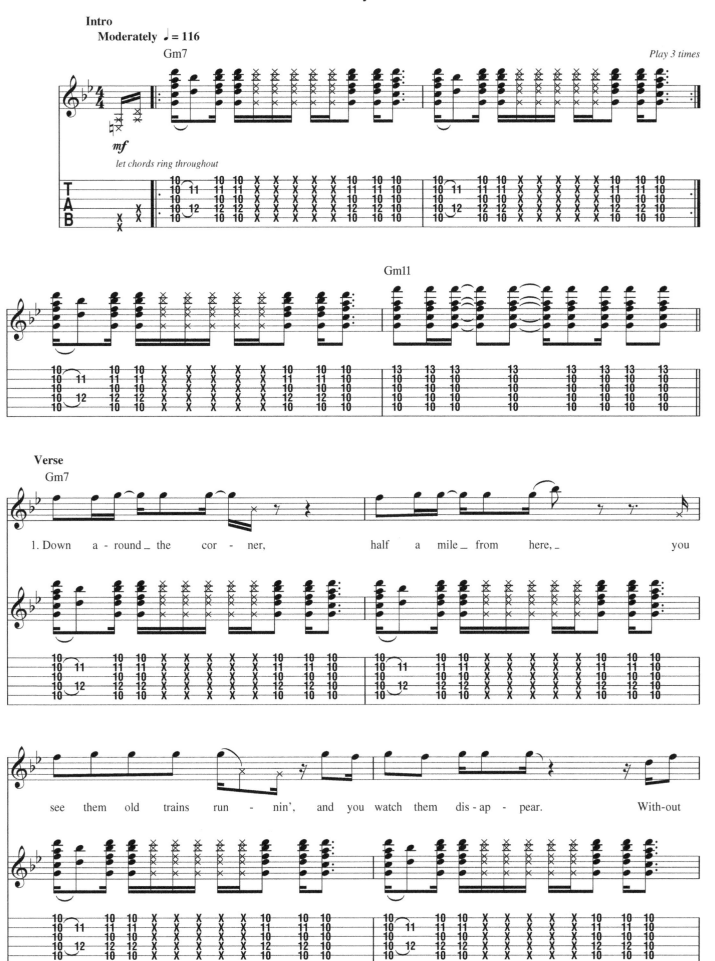

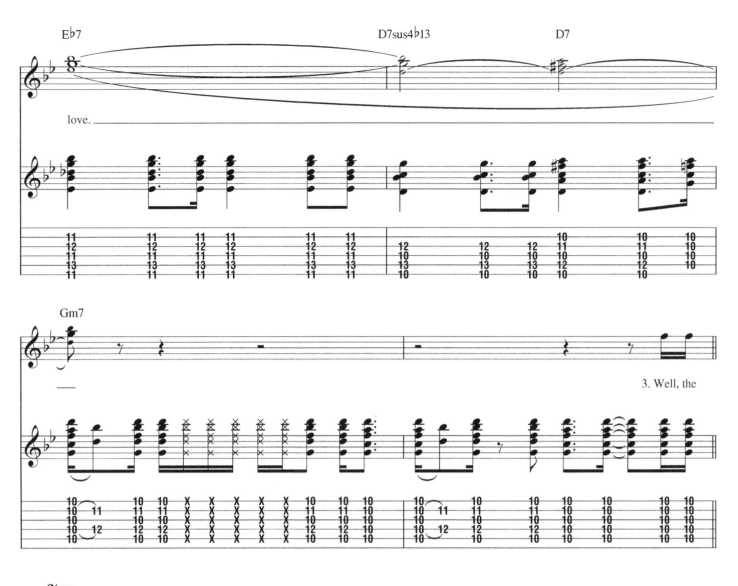

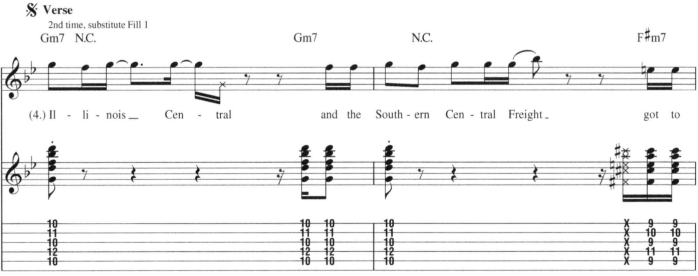

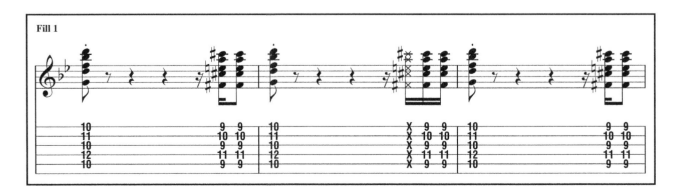

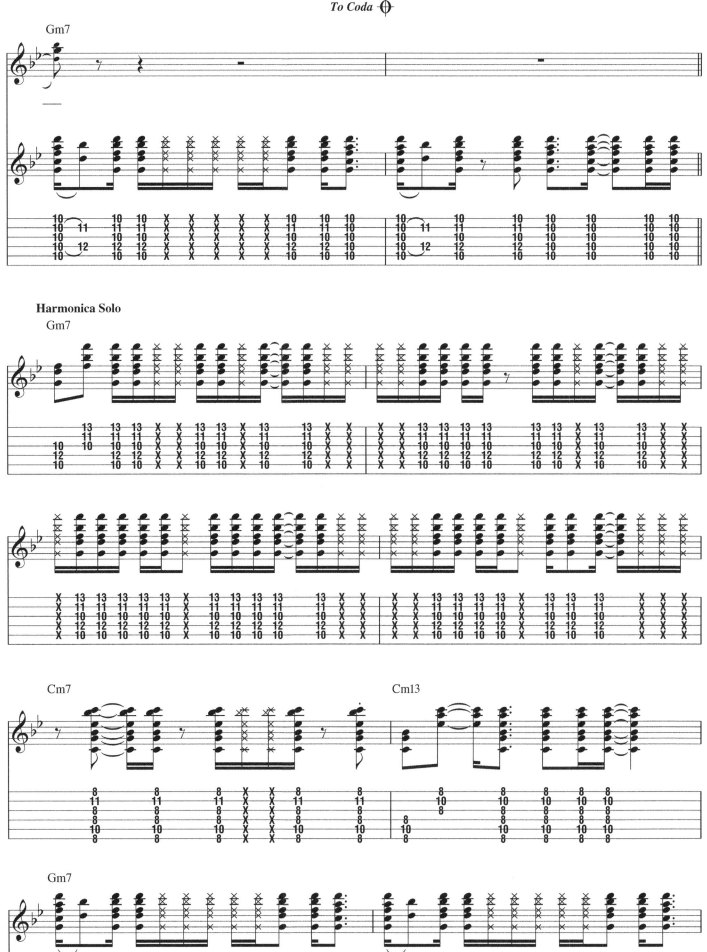

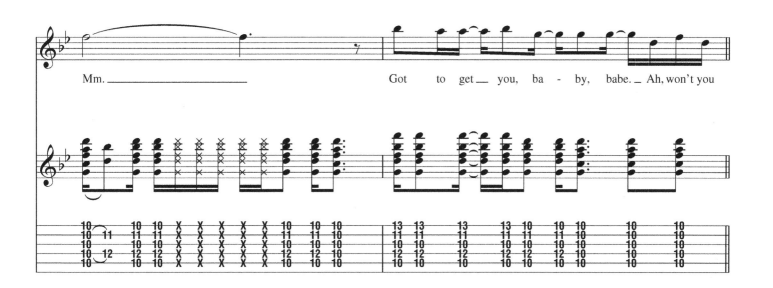

Mm. _____ Got to get _ you, ba - by, babe. _ Ah, won't you

Gm7

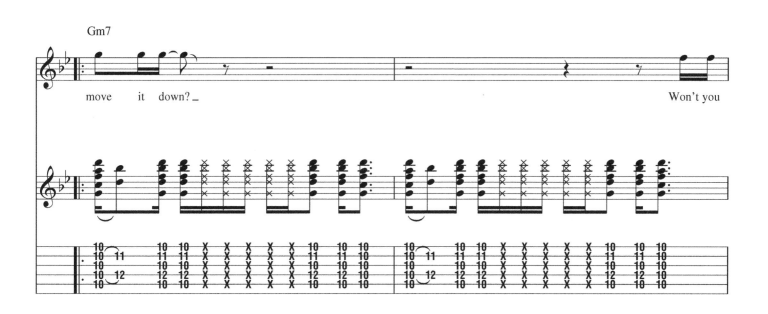

move it down? _ Won't you

Repeat and fade

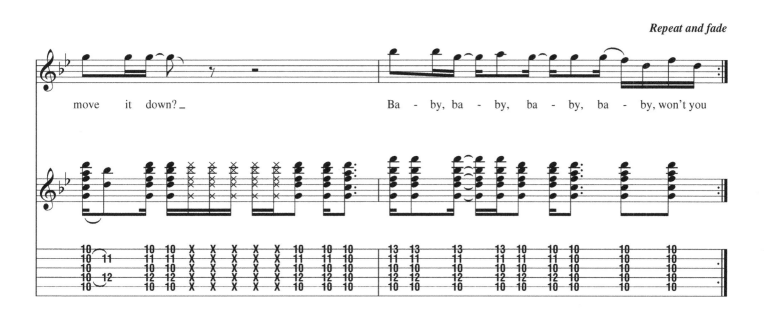

move it down? _ Ba - by, ba - by, ba - by, ba - by, won't you

South City Midnight Lady

Words and Music by Patrick Simmons

Open G tuning:
(low to high) D-G-D-G-B-D

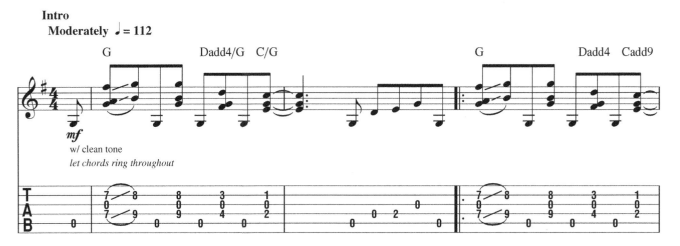

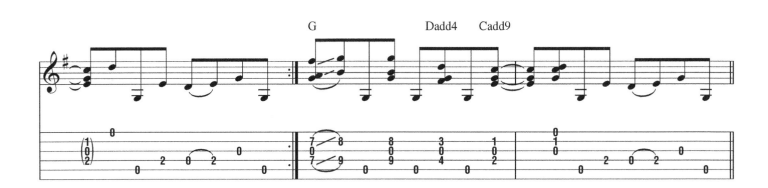

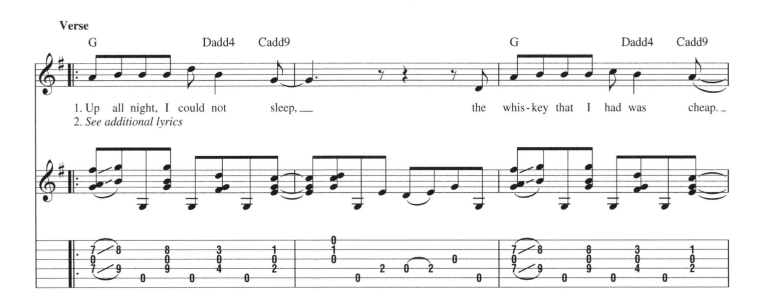

Chorus

3rd time, substitute Fill 1

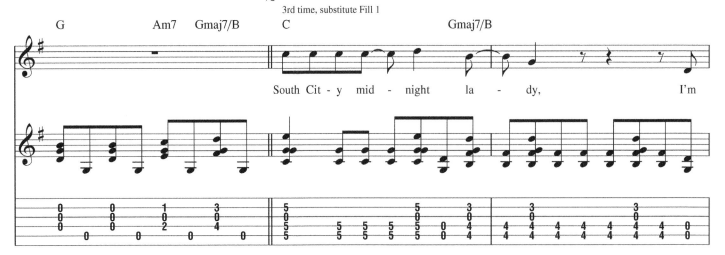

South Cit - y mid - night la - dy, I'm

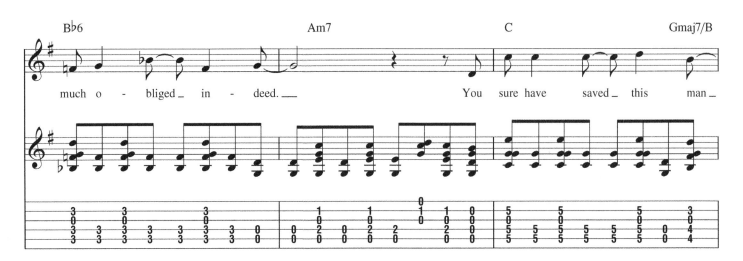

much o - bliged __ in - deed. __ You sure have saved __ this man __

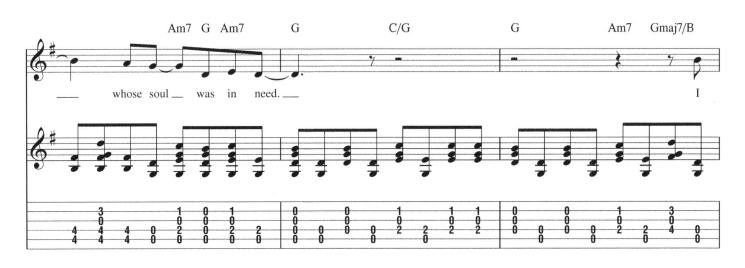

__ whose soul __ was in need. __ I

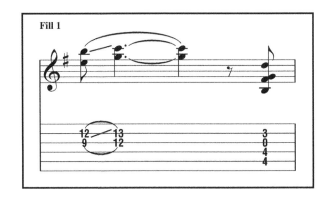

Fill 1

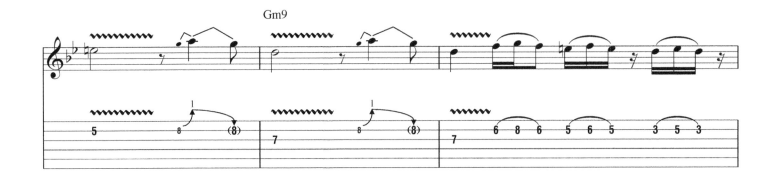

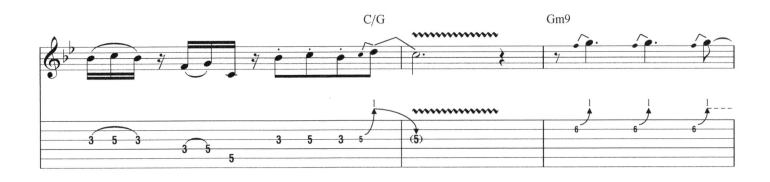

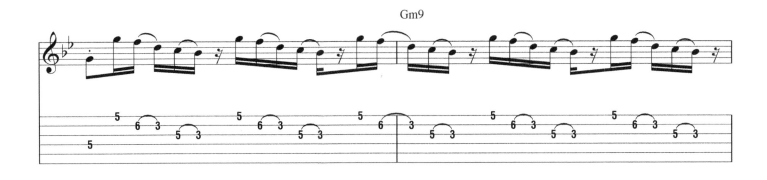

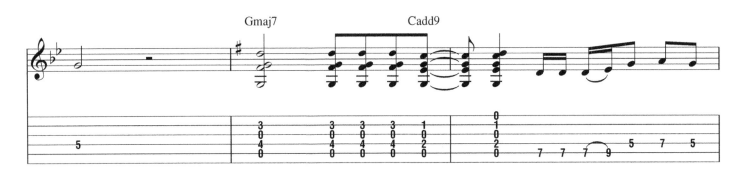

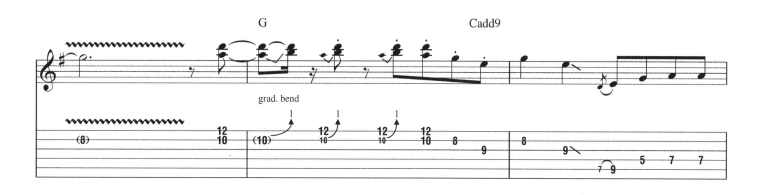

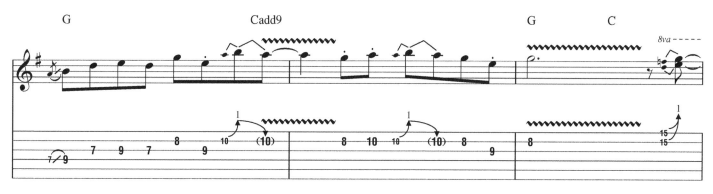

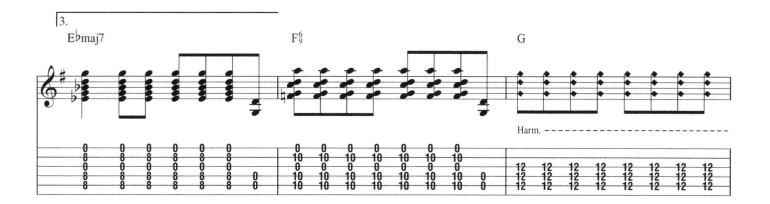

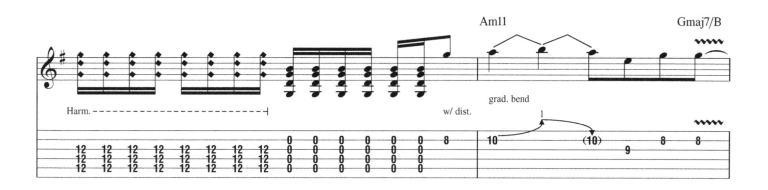

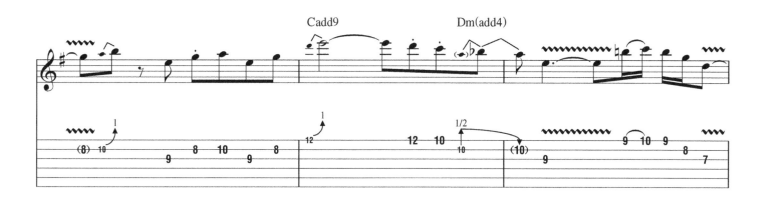

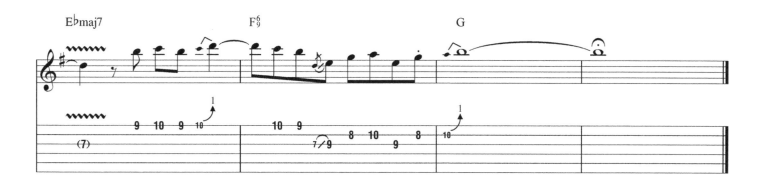

Additional Lyrics

2. When day has left the night behind,
   And shadows roll across my mind,
   I sometimes find myself alone out walking the street.
   Yes, and when I'm feelin' down and blue,
   Then all I do is think of you,
   And all my foolish problems seem to fade away.

Rockin' Down the Highway

Words and Music by Tom Johnston

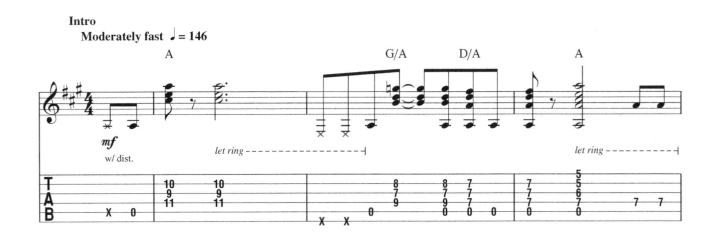

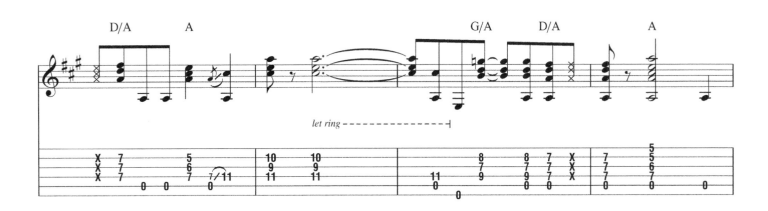

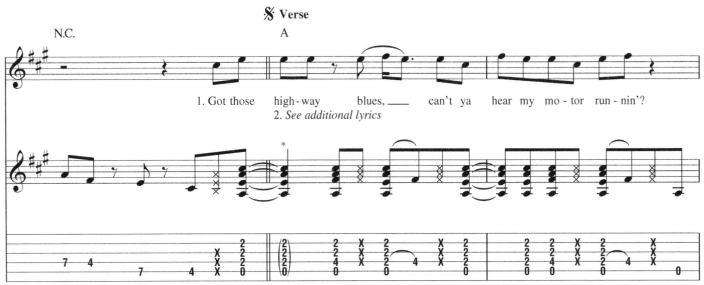

1. Got those high-way blues, ___ can't ya hear my mo-tor run-nin'?
2. *See additional lyrics*

*Strike chord on repeat.

*T = Thumb on 6th string.

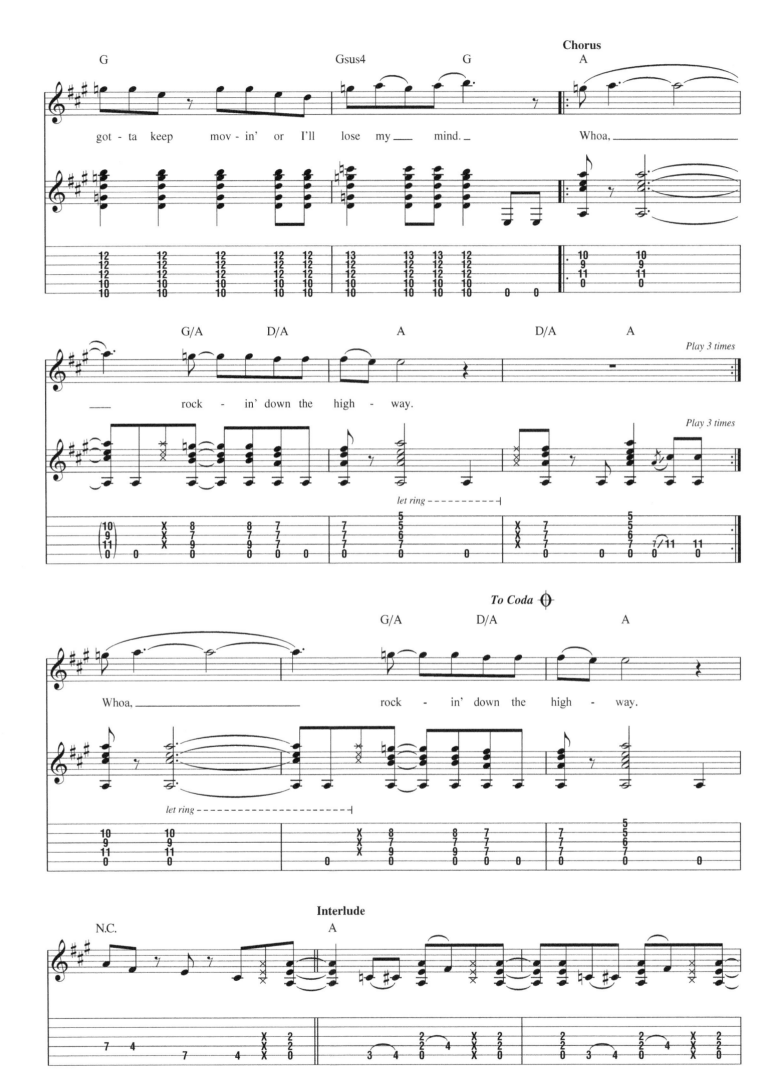

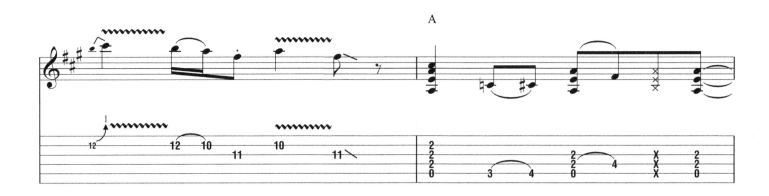

Guitar Solo

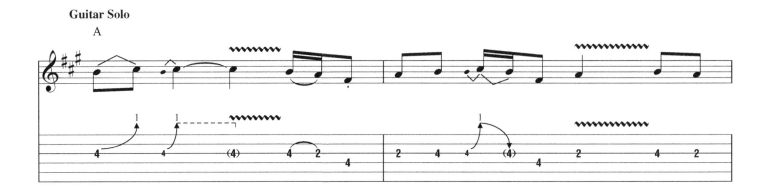

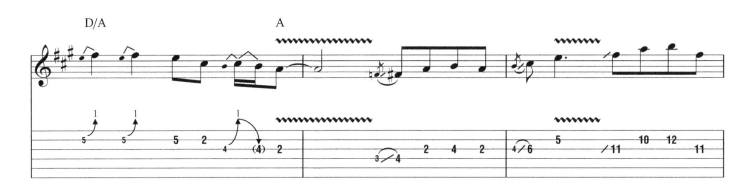

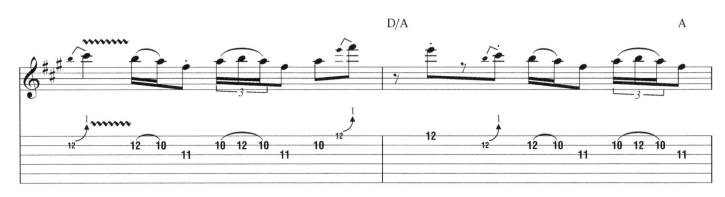

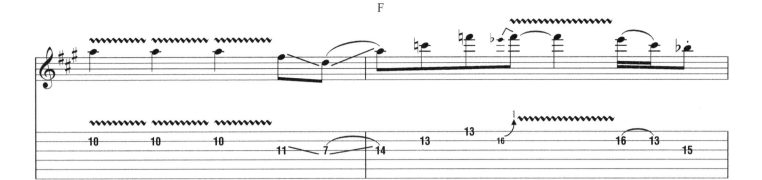

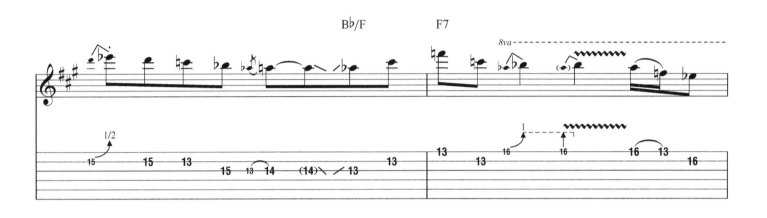

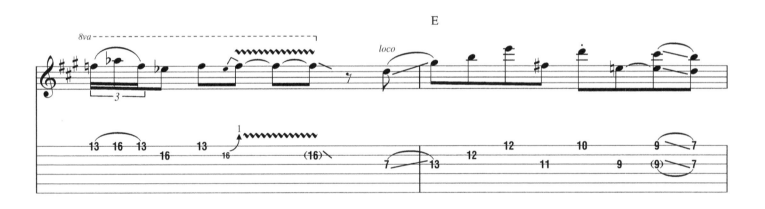

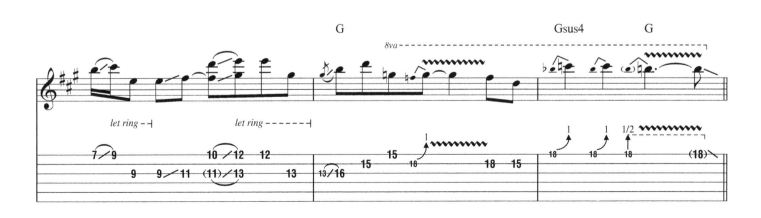

Outro-Chorus

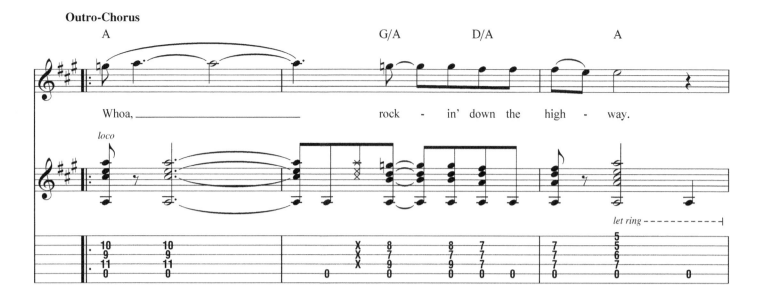

Whoa, _____ rock - in' down the high - way.

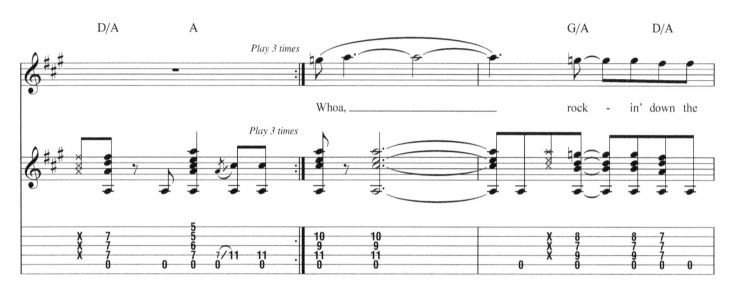

Whoa, _____ rock - in' down the

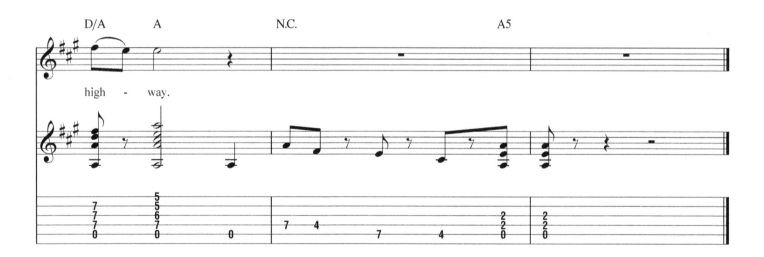

high - way.

Additional Lyrics

2. The highway patrol got his eyes on me.
   I know what he's thinkin' and it ain't good.
   I'm movin' so fast he can barely see me.
   Gonna lose that man, I know I should.

Pre-Chorus I gotta kick in my pedal,
   Make my Ford move a little bit faster.
   Can't stop, and I can't stop,
   Gotta keep movin' or I'll lose my mind.

Takin' It to the Streets

Words and Music by Michael McDonald

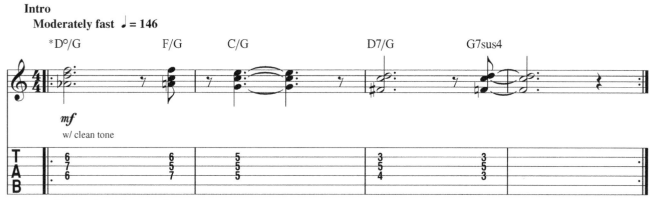

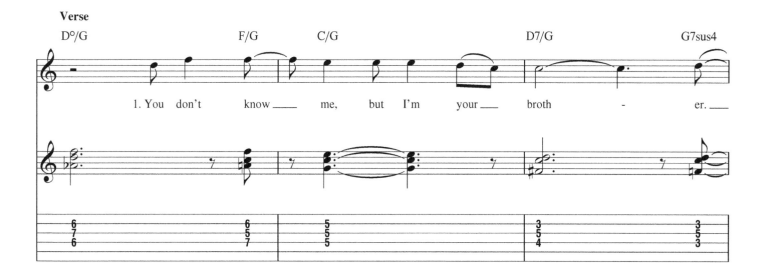

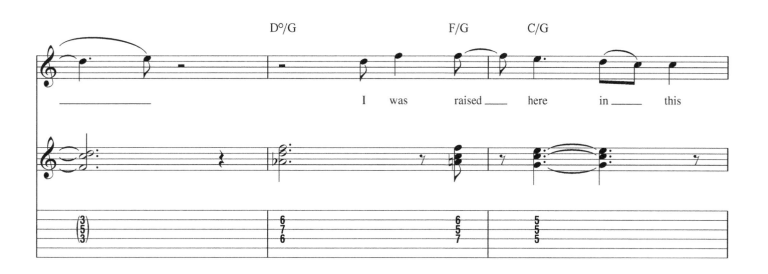

GUITAR NOTATION LEGEND

THE MUSICAL STAFF shows pitches and rhythms and is divided by bar lines into measures. Pitches are named after the first seven letters of the alphabet.

TABLATURE graphically represents the guitar fingerboard. Each horizontal line represents a string, and each number represents a fret.

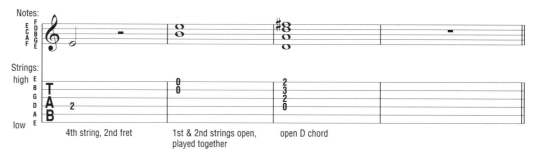

4th string, 2nd fret

1st & 2nd strings open, played together

open D chord

HALF-STEP BEND: Strike the note and bend up 1/2 step.

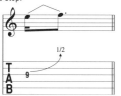

WHOLE-STEP BEND: Strike the note and bend up one step.

GRACE NOTE BEND: Strike the note and immediately bend up as indicated.

SLIGHT (MICROTONE) BEND: Strike the note and bend up 1/4 step.

BEND AND RELEASE: Strike the note and bend up as indicated, then release back to the original note. Only the first note is struck.

PRE-BEND: Bend the note as indicated, then strike it.

VIBRATO: The string is vibrated by rapidly bending and releasing the note with the fretting hand.

PALM MUTING: The note is partially muted by the pick hand lightly touching the string(s) just before the bridge.

HAMMER-ON: Strike the first (lower) note with one finger, then sound the higher note (on the same string) with another finger by fretting it without picking.

PULL-OFF: Place both fingers on the notes to be sounded. Strike the first note and without picking, pull the finger off to sound the second (lower) note.

LEGATO SLIDE: Strike the first note and then slide the same fret-hand finger up or down to the second note. The second note is not struck.

SHIFT SLIDE: Same as legato slide, except the second note is struck.

TRILL: Very rapidly alternate between the notes indicated by continuously hammering on and pulling off.

TAPPING: Hammer ("tap") the fret indicated with the pick-hand index or middle finger and pull off to the note fretted by the fret hand.

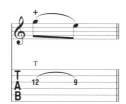

NATURAL HARMONIC: Strike the note while the fret-hand lightly touches the string directly over the fret indicated.

PINCH HARMONIC: The note is fretted normally and a harmonic is produced by adding the edge of the thumb or the tip of the index finger of the pick hand to the normal pick attack.

TREMOLO PICKING: The note is picked as rapidly and continuously as possible.

VIBRATO BAR DIVE AND RETURN: The pitch of the note or chord is dropped a specified number of steps (in rhythm), then returned to the original pitch.

VIBRATO BAR SCOOP: Depress the bar just before striking the note, then quickly release the bar.

VIBRATO BAR DIP: Strike the note and then immediately drop a specified number of steps, then release back to the original pitch.

Additional Musical Definitions

(accent) • Accentuate note (play it louder).

(staccato) • Play the note short.

D.S. al Coda • Go back to the sign (%), then play until the measure marked "*To Coda*," then skip to the section labelled "**Coda**."

D.C. al Fine • Go back to the beginning of the song and play until the measure marked "*Fine*" (end).

Fill • Label used to identify a brief melodic figure which is to be inserted into the arrangement.

N.C. • Harmony is implied.

• Repeat measures between signs.

• When a repeated section has different endings, play the first ending only the first time and the second ending only the second time.

This series will help you play your favorite songs quickly and easily. Just follow the tab and listen to the audio to hear how the guitar should sound, and then play along using the separate backing tracks.

Playback tools are provided for slowing down the tempo without changing pitch and looping challenging parts. The melody and lyrics are included in the book so that you can sing or simply follow along.

107. CREAM
00701069.............................$17.99

108. THE WHO
00701053.............................$17.99

109. STEVE MILLER
00701054.............................$19.99

110. SLIDE GUITAR HITS
00701055.............................$17.99

111. JOHN MELLENCAMP
00701056.............................$14.99

112. QUEEN
00701052.............................$16.99

113. JIM CROCE
00701058.............................$19.99

114. BON JOVI
00701060.............................$17.99

115. JOHNNY CASH
00701070.............................$17.99

116. THE VENTURES
00701124.............................$17.99

117. BRAD PAISLEY
00701224.............................$16.99

118. ERIC JOHNSON
00701353.............................$17.99

119. AC/DC CLASSICS
00701356.............................$19.99

120. PROGRESSIVE ROCK
00701457.............................$14.99

121. U2
00701508.............................$17.99

122. CROSBY, STILLS & NASH
00701610.............................$16.99

123. LENNON & McCARTNEY ACOUSTIC
00701614.............................$16.99

124. SMOOTH JAZZ
00200664.............................$16.99

125. JEFF BECK
00701687.............................$19.99

126. BOB MARLEY
00701701.............................$17.99

127. 1970S ROCK
00701739.............................$17.99

128. 1960S ROCK
00701740.............................$14.99

129. MEGADETH
00701741.............................$17.99

130. IRON MAIDEN
00701742.............................$17.99

131. 1990S ROCK
00701743.............................$14.99

132. COUNTRY ROCK
00701757.............................$15.99

133. TAYLOR SWIFT
00701894.............................$16.99

135. MINOR BLUES
00151350.............................$17.99

136. GUITAR THEMES
00701922.............................$14.99

137. IRISH TUNES
00701966.............................$15.99

138. BLUEGRASS CLASSICS
00701967.............................$17.99

139. GARY MOORE
00702370.............................$17.99

140. MORE STEVIE RAY VAUGHAN
00702396.............................$19.99

141. ACOUSTIC HITS
00702401.............................$16.99

142. GEORGE HARRISON
00237697.............................$17.99

143. SLASH
00702425.............................$19.99

144. DJANGO REINHARDT
00702531.............................$17.99

145. DEF LEPPARD
00702532.............................$19.99

146. ROBERT JOHNSON
00702533.............................$16.99

147. SIMON & GARFUNKEL
14041591.............................$17.99

148. BOB DYLAN
14041592.............................$17.99

149. AC/DC HITS
14041593.............................$19.99

150. ZAKK WYLDE
02501717.............................$19.99

151. J.S. BACH
02501730.............................$16.99

152. JOE BONAMASSA
02501751.............................$24.99

153. RED HOT CHILI PEPPERS
00702990.............................$22.99

155. ERIC CLAPTON – FROM THE ALBUM UNPLUGGED
00703085 ....$17.99

156. SLAYER
00703770.............................$19.99

157. FLEETWOOD MAC
00101382.............................$17.99

159. WES MONTGOMERY
00102593.............................$22.99

160. T-BONE WALKER
00102641.............................$17.99

161. THE EAGLES – ACOUSTIC
00102659.............................$19.99

162. THE EAGLES HITS
00102667.............................$17.99

163. PANTERA
00103036.............................$19.99

164. VAN HALEN 1986-1995
00110270.............................$19.99

165. GREEN DAY
00210343.............................$17.99

166. MODERN BLUES
00700764.............................$16.99

167. DREAM THEATER
00111938.............................$24.99

168. KISS
00113421.............................$17.99

169. TAYLOR SWIFT
00115982.............................$16.99

170. THREE DAYS GRACE
00117337.............................$16.99

171. JAMES BROWN
00117420.............................$16.99

172. THE DOOBIE BROTHERS
00119670.............................$17.99

173. TRANS-SIBERIAN ORCHESTRA
00119907.............................$19.99

174. SCORPIONS
00122119.............................$19.99

175. MICHAEL SCHENKER
00122127.............................$17.99

176. BLUES BREAKERS WITH JOHN MAYALL & ERIC CLAPTON
00122132.............................$19.99

177. ALBERT KING
00123271.............................$17.99

178. JASON MRAZ
00124165.............................$17.99

179. RAMONES
00127073.............................$16.99

180. BRUNO MARS
00129706.............................$16.99

181. JACK JOHNSON
00129854.............................$16.99

182. SOUNDGARDEN
00138161.............................$17.99

183. BUDDY GUY
00138240.............................$17.99

184. KENNY WAYNE SHEPHERD
00138258.............................$17.99

185. JOE SATRIANI
00139457.............................$19.99

186. GRATEFUL DEAD
00139459.............................$17.99

187. JOHN DENVER
00140839.............................$19.99

188. MÖTLEY CRUE
00141145.............................$19.99

189. JOHN MAYER
00144350.............................$19.99

190. DEEP PURPLE
00146152.............................$19.99

191. PINK FLOYD CLASSICS
00146164.............................$17.99

192. JUDAS PRIEST
00151352.............................$19.99

193. STEVE VAI
00156028.............................$19.99

194. PEARL JAM
00157925.............................$17.99

195. METALLICA: 1983-1988
00234291.............................$22.99

196. METALLICA: 1991-2016
00234292.............................$19.99

HAL•LEONARD®

For complete songlists, visit
Hal Leonard online at
www.halleonard.com

Prices, contents, and availability subject to
change without notice.